INT.

INTERNATIONAL

FAITH ON THE MOVE

A DEVOTIONAL FOR MK/TCK TEENS IN CROSS-CULTURAL TRANSITION

Discounted rates available for orders of 10 or more
Faith on the Move books. Learn more at:
www.interactionintl.org

Faith on the Move: A Devotional for MK/TCK Teens in Cross-Cultural Transition
(c) 2022 by Interaction International

Edited by David Abernathy with Tarrah Grabler and Rachel Hicks
Designed by Holly Baldwin
Cover Photo from Canva.com, Getty Images Pro: Natalia Deriabina
Daily photos and graphics from Canva.com

ISBN: 9798425166494

For more information about Interaction International, visit our website
www.interactionintl.org.

PRAISE FOR FAITH ON THE MOVE

Physical transition is nothing new. Ever since Adam and Eve sinned and were cast out of the only world they knew, humans have had to deal with the effects of transition. Through these stories and writings of others, we are reminded that the same God who was faithful to them is with us today. The practical applications at the end of each lesson make this a book both encouraging and instructive in our fast-changing world.

Ruth E. Van Reken

Adult TCK, co-author of *Third Culture Kids: Growing Up Among Worlds*, co-founder Families in Global Transition

Insightful and incredibly useful guide to accompany TCKs on their journey through transition. It weaves the experiences of TCKs into the wider story of God's love. It's both practical and relatable; I'm excited this tool exists.

Christopher O'Shaughnessy

Adult Military Kid, International Speaker, and Author of *Arrivals, Departures and the Adventures In-Between*

I wish it wasn't so short! This book was written for us, not monoculturals! So if you're tired of going through devotionals that don't address the pain of saying goodbye every three years or the awkward cultural blunders you make, read this.

Breanna Woodson

Teen MK, Uganda/USA

Faith on the Move is a must-read daily devotional. Written for TCKs, you'll find your soul resonates while reading. From one TCK to another...use this devo to start your day!

Paul Dyck

Adult MK, MORE Network Ambassador

I wish I could have read this book as an MK teen in the 1960s–70s and shared it with my own TCK teens in the 1990s–2000s. It was challenging and helpful for me, an aging ATCK, and I commend the book to anyone at any stage of their TCK journey.

Dr. John Barclay
Adult MK, Education & TCK Consultant

I am a highly skeptical person of devotionals, but this one was actually really good. I am older than the target audience and I still felt it was quite relevant to some of the cultural aspects of transition that I am processing.

Riley Edey
Adult TCK, Ireland/Scotland/Canada

The question about what cultural compromises/adaptations am I willing to make and what spiritual convictions am I unwilling to compromise really struck me. I'm not a teenager anymore but I have an upcoming cross-cultural move and I will be reading these.

Haddie Grace
Adult TCK, Africa/USA

This devotional is perfect for transitioning to another country. It walks you through all the pivotal thoughts and emotions, and helps you develop strategies to make the transition smoother. I highly recommend it for anyone in the process of transitioning.

Titus McFadden
Teen MK, Asia/USA

A good resource for TCKs going through cross-cultural transition. Each reading is filled with powerful prayers, quotes, and Bible passages.

"J"
Teen TCK, Asia/USA

INTRODUCTION

One summer after running an Interaction International cross-cultural transition seminar (Transit Lounge), my mind was filled with conversations I had with the MKs/TCKs who attended. They were processing their mobile, global identity and the goodbyes they had just said. They wondered how their transitions to their passport country (where their parents called home) would play out as they headed to high school, college, or a gap year experience.

During Transit Lounge that summer, we had morning devotionals based on some of the TCKs of Scripture: Ruth, Joseph, Esther, and Daniel. Those Biblical TCKs faced some challenges similar to the ones the MKs/TCKs at our seminar experience and yet God used them in amazing ways.

So, I wrote this devotional for you as you continue to process your MK/TCK journey. You can use this on your own or with a group of friends. My hope is that this devotional will deepen your walk with Christ and speak to the issues you face during transition. This is especially true for those of you who are starting college or taking a gap year and are looking for a church.

The words of the Apostle Paul in Ephesians 3:16-19 capture my prayer for each of you:

"I pray that out of his glorious riches he may strengthen you with power through his Spirit in your inner being, so that Christ may dwell in your hearts through faith. And I pray that you, being rooted and established in love, may have power, together with all the Lord's holy people, to grasp how wide and long and high and deep is the love of Christ, and to know this love that surpasses knowledge—that you may be filled to the measure of all the fullness of God."

Blessings,

Janet Blomberg
*Executive Director of Interaction International (2005-2018)
and former Editor of Interact Magazine*

Join a Book Group

Two are better than one,
because they have a good return for their labor:
If either of them falls down,
one can help the other up.
But pity anyone who falls
and has no one to help them up.
Also, if two lie down together, they will keep warm.
But how can one keep warm alone?
Though one may be overpowered,
two can defend themselves.
A cord of three strands is not quickly broken.

Ecclesiastes 4:9–12

Interaction International believes community is crucial for health —especially in the midst of a cross-cultural transition. We know community is often difficult to find during those times. If you are looking to find a community of MKs/TCKs to journey with you through reading *Faith on the Move*, we invite you to fill out an interest form by scanning the QR code below or going to interactionintl.org/publications/faith-on-the-move.

PSALM 139:9-10

IF I RISE ON THE WINGS OF THE DAWN,
IF I SETTLE ON THE FAR SIDE OF THE SEA,
EVEN THERE YOUR HAND WILL GUIDE ME,
YOUR RIGHT HAND WILL HOLD ME FAST.

Dedicated to the One to Whom we can entrust our roots;
our Anchor; our Constant.

RUTH

FROM MOAB TO BETHLEHEM

Sea of Chinnereth

NORTH

Golan

+ Mount Carmel
Elijah's contest
with Baal's
prophets

Mount Tabor
+ Deborah and Barak

Edrei

Ramoth-gilead

Saul and Jonathan slain

Samaria

Shechem
Law read between
two mountains

Jabbok River

Jordan River

Mahanaim
Absalom killed
River
Peniel
Jacob wrestles angel

Shiloh

Jacob's ladder vision
Bethel
Ophrah
Mizpah
Ai
Achan's sin
causes defeat
Gilgal
Beth-Horon
Jericho
Walls collapse
Rabbah

Ammonites

valley
sun still for Joshua
Gibeah

Jerusalem
Melchizedek blesses
Abraham at Salem
Bethlehem
Ruth marries Boaz
Abraham offers Isaac
at Mount Moriah
Heshbon

Mount
Nebo +
Moses dies
Bezer

Jahaz

Adullam
David hides
from Saul

Hebron

Salt

Sea

Arnon River

Amorites

Beersheba
Esau gives Jacob his birthright
Hormah

Moabites

Sodom (?)
Sodom and Gomorrah destroyed
Zoar
Brook
Zered
Edomites

DAY 1 - RUTH: LOSSES AND HOPE

Read Ruth 1:16-17

Key Verse: *But Ruth replied, "Don't urge me to leave you or to turn back from you. Where you go I will go, and where you stay I will stay. Your people will be my people and your God my God."* **Ruth 1:16**

A Prayer of St. Teresa of Avila

Holy God, Blessed Trinity,
let me always be rooted in you
so that I may live in you and you in me.
Bless me so that your grace may flow through me,
allowing me to bear your fruit to a hungry and helpless world.

As I wander, prune me of all that inhibits your growth in me.
Let me do nothing apart from you
so that your joy may be complete in me.
In Christ's name I pray.
Amen.

Reflections

Ruth lost it all! She lost her family and friends, her home culture, and everything that was familiar to her. Because of her decision to go with Naomi to Bethlehem, she faced the challenges of entering an unfamiliar culture where everything was new. Though noble, her decision didn't make her transition easy. Thankfully, her story didn't end with the chaos of transition, but with friendship, belonging, and love.

Comedians make fun of mothers-in-law. They're portrayed as being meddling, bossy, and interfering. While this is a common stereotype, it was not the reality for Ruth. Her mother-in-law, Naomi, had a profound effect on every area of her life and was her culture bridge, mentor, and matchmaker. She guided Ruth through the tough times as well as the joyous ones. They supported, encouraged, and challenged one another in each stage of their lives.

Hopefully you've had people who have had a profound effect on you. People who were there for you when you faced hard goodbyes or reached out and welcomed you when you were the hidden immigrant. Maybe someone who was encouraging and gave you a sense of belonging when you were lonely. They were not there by accident; God put them in your life and He will add new people during this transition to be your helpers and encouragers.

Questions
- *Who are some of the key people in your life?*
- *What did they do that made such a difference to you?*
- *How did God use them?*
- *What can you learn about being an encourager in someone else's life?*
- *What else is God saying to you through this passage?*

Next Steps
1. Let someone know (whether through text, call, email, etc.) how much you appreciated them at the important times in your life.
2. Reach out to someone with an act of help or encouragement.
3. Pray that God would bring those important people into your new life and that He would make you that person for someone else.

DAY 2 - RUTH: FORCED TO GO

Read Ruth 1:1–3

Key Verse: *In the days when the judges ruled, there was a famine in the land. So a man from Bethlehem in Judah, together with his wife and two sons, went to live for a while in the country of Moab.* **Ruth 1:1**

31 Days of Praise - Day 18

Thank You that each difficulty is an opportunity to see You work . . . that in Your time You will bring me out to a place of abundance. I rejoice that You plan to enrich and beautify me through each problem, each conflict, each struggle . . . that through them You expose my weaknesses and needs, my hidden sins, my self-centeredness (and especially my self-reliance and pride). Thank You that You use trials to humble me and perfect my faith and produce in me the quality of endurance . . . that they prepare the soil of my heart for the fresh new growth in godliness that You and I both long to see in me. [1]

Reflections

Life events and disasters can blindside you with no warning and no time to prepare. We like to pretend that we have control of our lives; that we know what to do today and what might be coming. Naomi, her husband, and sons each had normal lives in Bethlehem, but famine hit and everything changed. The city whose name meant "the house of bread" no longer had any food!

For many of you, your transitions have all been planned for and expected months in advance. However, many of you have experienced transitions that came suddenly, without warning and due to circumstances beyond your control or your family's control. Instead of famine, you faced civil war, terrorism, acts of violence, medical or family emergencies, or something equally shocking that hit in an instant and forced you and your family to leave.

Those sudden goodbyes can often feel like rips in your life. Where a chapter should have ended there are only torn pages. If that's how you feel, it's okay. You're not alone and you can recover.

Questions

- *Have you had a forced transition? How did you deal with it or respond to it?*
- *Are there any aspects of that transition that are still unresolved? (e.g., resentment, anger, sadness, confusion, etc.)*
- *Even if you haven't had a sudden transition, are there ways that past transitions are affecting your present?*
- *What else is God saying to you through this passage?*

Next Steps

1. Pray for God's peace and guidance for those involved in forced transitions.
2. If you have people to forgive, ask God how to surrender this and let it go. If you have people to grieve for, give yourself some space and time to grieve.
3. When talking with your other TCK friends, be sensitive that this may be a part of their story. Some can go back; others can't. Be aware of this and ready to be supportive.

DAY 3 - RUTH: SETTLING IN

Read Ruth 1:4

Key Verse: *They married Moabite women, one named Orpah and the other Ruth.* **Ruth 1:4a**

Mark and Jill Herringshaw

Father, I thank You that You have not called me Your servant, but rather Your friend. Thank You that Jesus modeled intimate friendship with His disciples, especially John, Peter, and James.

My season of life has changed . . . I am longing for a godly friend who will walk with me towards the life to which Jesus has called us.

Would you please lead me to a new friend? One who fits all the criteria David outlines in Psalm 101 – one who seeks Your ways? Make me worthy of one such friend by being that very kind of person myself . . . Grant me favor and make me a magnet for godly people so that I can grow my circle of friendship to one that gives You glory and much joy. In Jesus' Name. Amen. [2]

Reflections

Naomi spent ten years living in Moab, not just a year or two. She didn't know when the famine would end, or when, if ever, she would return to Bethlehem. She had no choice but to move forward with life in Moab. She built new relationships and went through the normal events of life there. There were weddings, and two daughters-in-law, Ruth and Orpah, were added to her family. There were funerals as Naomi's husband and two sons died. There was a closeness to Naomi's relationships with both Ruth and Orpah. Each of them knew what it was like to lose a husband. While they had laughed together and known great joy, they had also cried together, grieved together, and shared each other's losses.

Your transition experience may feel a lot like that. You don't know how long it will be before you can go home again, and that may seem scary. There's so much that you miss already! You're in the process of figuring out how this culture operates, how your school works, and how to function here. You're facing the challenge of saying "hello" to people and starting to build new friendships. You know that you're here long enough that you can't "camp out" for that long.

Questions
- *Where are you in this cycle? Are you open to new friendships? Are you grieving? Are you building new relationships?*
- *What steps can you take to move forward in this process and avoid getting stuck?*
- *What else is God saying to you through this passage?*

Next Steps
1. Make one attempt to get to know someone new where you are living.
2. Make one attempt to reconnect with someone you care about.

DAY 4 - RUTH: UPS AND DOWNS

Read Ruth 1:4-14

Key Verse: *After they had lived there about ten years, both Mahlon and Kilion also died, and Naomi was left without her two sons and her husband.* **Ruth 1:4-5**

Prayerist

"Be merciful to me, Lord, for I am in distress; my eyes grow weak with sorrow, my soul and body with grief" (Psalm 31:9, NIV). My heart is broken, my mind exhausted. I cry out to you and hardly know what to ask. All I can do is tell you how I feel and ask you to "keep track of all my sorrows. . . . [collect] all my tears in your bottle. . . . [and record] each one in your book" as I pour them out to you (Psalm 56:8, NLT).

Amen. [3]

Reflections

Transition is never linear; it's a process that unfortunately feels like one step forward then two steps back. Naomi took steps forward to settle into life in Moab and adapt to its culture. She may have felt that she was making progress in settling into the culture and making friends, but all the time there was the undercurrent of missing Bethlehem and life there. I'm certain there were times when she was suddenly reminded of all she had lost. She may have even thought that she was getting over those feelings when a new wave of grief and loss hit her.

This is just the way transition operates. It's not something we deal with once and it's done. There are always reminders (triggers) that unexpectedly bring back the things we have lost. Grief can suddenly surprise us. Your trigger may be a song, a smell, a food, connecting with a friend, seeing a story on the news, or nearly anything else. Transition is a dance mixed with moving forward, pausing, and even stepping backwards.

Questions

- *What losses are you feeling most right now?*
- *Have you been blindsided by something recently?*
- *What things have been triggers for you? How have you responded to them?*
- *What else is God saying to you through this passage?*

Next Steps

1. Cry out to God in those moments of shock.
2. Take one practical step to avoid or deal with one trigger.
3. Find another MK/TCK (whether face-to-face or virtually) and share with them your story about being blindsided.

DAY 5 - RUTH: WHAT'D I DO WRONG?

Read Ruth 1:15-22

Key Verse: *So Naomi returned from Moab accompanied by Ruth the Moabite, her daughter-in-law, arriving in Bethlehem as the barley harvest was beginning.*
Ruth 1:22

Jill Briscoe

*"Because you listened to me, I knew you loved me.
Because I knew you loved me, I listened to you."* [4]

Reflections

When Ruth married Naomi's son, she stepped out of Moab's culture and everything it represented and chose to embrace Naomi's Israelite culture, its values, and its God. When the famine ended, Naomi announced she was returning to Bethlehem. Ruth faced a life-changing choice: stay in Moab or go to unfamiliar Bethlehem. It was not an easy choice. If she went, Ruth would have to learn a new culture and mistakes would be inevitable. One of the best things to help with those mistakes is a mentor. Fortunately, Ruth had someone she could trust. Ruth had seen her handle problems as severe as the death of her husband and sons. Naomi could guide her.

Ruth was entering a new culture, and you've come to a culture that is supposed to be home (according to your passport), but isn't yet. You've probably already made some cultural blunders and they likely won't be the last, but you're not alone. Everyone makes them and they are a normal part of the transition process. An important thing to remember is that when those mistakes happen, you learn from them and move on. Most of the time they eventually become something to laugh at. They won't follow you forever.

Questions
- *What cultural mistakes have you made and how have you responded to them?*
- *Ruth had a mentor in Naomi. If you had a cultural/ spiritual mentor what qualities would you want that person to have?*
- *How will you identify those qualities in someone?*
- *What else is God saying to you through this passage?*

Next Steps
1. Say a quick prayer right now that God would help you find someone to support you through cultural mistakes and adjustments of transition.
2. List five qualities you are looking for in a cultural mentor and in a spiritual mentor.
3. Start a list of possible cultural mentors and spiritual mentors.

DAY 6 - RUTH: SAME BUT DIFFERENT

Read Ruth 1:19

Key Verse: *So the two women went on until they came to Bethlehem. When they arrived in Bethlehem, the whole town was stirred because of them, and the women exclaimed, "Can this be Naomi?"* **Ruth 1:19**

Prayer for Families, *Book of Common Prayer*

Almighty God, our heavenly Father, who settest the solitary in families: We commend to thy continual care the homes in which thy people dwell. Put far from them, we beseech thee, every root of bitterness, the desire of vainglory, and the pride of life. Fill them with faith, virtue, knowledge, temperance, patience, godliness. Knit together in constant affection those who, in holy wedlock, have been made one flesh. Turn the hearts of the parents to the children, and the hearts of the children to the parents; and so enkindle fervent charity among us all, that we may evermore be kindly affectioned one to another; through Jesus Christ our Lord. Amen. [5]

Reflections

Naomi returned to Bethlehem, but she wasn't the same person as when she left. She'd learned what was expected and how to act in Moab. She likely made friends, had a sense of belonging and felt at home there. However, when she returned to Bethlehem, everyone was asking, "Is this Naomi?" She had changed and so had they. Life had gone on without her.

Returning to the country of your passport, you may have expected to fit in with extended family or friends. After all, they're family! You thought they would understand you and that you would feel connected to them. However, over time things have been said or done that made you feel disconnected. You may have returned to churches or places where you had been before and it just isn't the same or what you expected. Perhaps you thought you would reconnect with a good friend, but they've made new friends and are excluding you. That hurts. You can grow together again just as you grew apart but that takes time and work. In the meantime you have to allow for change.

Questions

- *Have you experienced distance and disconnectedness in relationships where you expected closeness and connection? How have you responded?*
- *Are there steps you can take to reach out or to build the relationship? How might things look from their perspective?*
- *What else is God saying to you through this passage?*

Next Steps

1. Pray for your relationships with extended family and friends, and for their other relationships.
2. Think about your plans for upcoming holidays such as Christmas or other breaks. Where will you stay and what will you do?

JOSEPH

FROM CANAAN TO EGYPT

DAY 7 - JOSEPH: PRISON TO PALACE

Read Genesis 45:4-8

Key Verse: *And now, do not be distressed and do not be angry with yourselves for selling me here, because it was to save lives that God sent me ahead of you.* **Genesis 45:5**

Oswald Chambers

Our yesterdays present irreparable things to us; it is true that we have lost opportunities which will never return, but God can transform this destructive anxiety into a constructive thoughtfulness for the future. Let the past sleep, but let it sleep in the bosom of Christ. [6]

Reflections

The story of Joseph is very familiar and filled with great highs and lows. It includes messy family relationships, feelings of betrayal, and being sold into slavery. It includes long years in prison and feeling forgotten. It includes adapting to a new culture and pressures inherent in the process. Although he faced hardship, Joseph became a great leader in Egypt with enormous power and prestige. His life models forgiving others, restoring relationships, and most of all, exhibiting a life of faith.

While the stories of your life may not be as dramatic as those of Joseph's life (or maybe they are), the themes are definitely similar. Throughout his life, Joseph repeatedly had to make choices about his actions, and each time, he demonstrated faith. At the end of his life, Joseph gave instructions concerning his bones, asking the Israelites not to leave him when they go to the Promised Land. In faith, he believed God would eventually bring His people out of Egypt as He had promised. Hundreds of years later, when God brought the Israelites out of Egypt, they remembered their promise and moved Joseph's bones to the Promised Land.

Questions

- *As you transition, how is God asking you to respond in faith, like Joseph?*
- *In your life as a TCK, what have been the highlights? What about the low points? How have they impacted your life of faith?*
- *What else is God saying to you through this passage?*

Next Steps

1. What promise from God do you need to remember in the midst of your transition?
2. Claim a promise from Scripture over your life in prayer today.
3. What do you need to trust God for right now?

18

DAY 8 - JOSEPH: FAMILY FEUDS

Read Genesis 37:1-11

Key Verse: *Joseph had a dream, and when he told it to his brothers, they hated him all the more.* **Genesis 37:5**

A Prayer of the Northumbria Community

May the peace of the Lord Christ go with you,
Wherever He may send you.
May He guide you through the wilderness,
Protect you through the storm.
May He bring you home rejoicing
At the wonders He has shown you.
May He bring you home rejoicing
Once again into our doors.

Reflections

When Joseph shared his dreams with his brothers, it got him into deep trouble. He was his father's favorite son and everyone knew it because of the coat he was given. His father dearly loved him, but his brothers were jealous and hated him. Emotions led to words, plans, and actions.

Joseph was part of a family and that can be a messy business. You have families too, and may have issues with your siblings, parents, or grandparents. No matter how wonderful your family is, no one's family can be perfect. In the midst of transition, these issues may come to the surface. The stress of transition may open old wounds or create new ones. Whether your family is near or far, your family will affect your transition. As you enter this culture, you may want to think about how your family is affecting you during this move.

Questions

- *What are the positive and negative dynamics in your family relationships?*
- *How is this transition affecting your family relationships?*
- *How does your proximity to (or distance from) your family affect this transition?*
- *What else is God saying to you through this passage?*

Next Steps

1. Pray for your family today.
2. Are there things that need to be forgiven? Make your apologies or tell someone you were hurt.
3. Every transition creates an opportunity for growth. What can you do to strengthen your family?

DAY 9 - JOSEPH: INJUSTICE

Read Genesis 37:12-36

Key Verse: *So when the Midianite merchants came by, his brothers pulled Joseph up out of the cistern and sold him for twenty shekels of silver to the Ishmaelites, who took him to Egypt.* **Genesis 37:28**

Ruth Bell Graham

Father, thank You for Your sovereign care. I praise You for working all things in my life for Your glory and my good. Help me to see the light of Your love when my path is painfully dark.

Reflections

Joseph's father asked him to go and check on his brothers, who were tending the flocks. Joseph obeyed and what happened next was not fair. He was thrown into a pit and sold into slavery. It was definitely a better option than being killed, but it was not a great experience. His father was lied to and was overwhelmed with grief thinking that Joseph was dead.

Life isn't fair. It wasn't fair when Joseph's brothers sold him into slavery and it isn't fair now. Injustice is woven into the fabric of every culture, and often it cuts the deepest when it surprises us. Whether the injustice is betrayal from those we trust, a failure of the system we believe in, or the decisions of others impacting our lives, part of us screams that things are not the way they should be. Life's unfair. You've got to wonder what Joseph thought when he was sold into slavery by his brothers. Did he accuse God of injustice? It would have been hard not to.

Questions

- *Are there things during your transition that you feel have been unfair? How have you reacted?*
- *Knowing the story of Joseph, would you say that he received justice in the end?*
- *Are there ways in which you have been unjust or unfair (e.g., toward individuals, groups, or cultures)?*
- *What else is God saying to you through this passage?*

Next Steps

1. Pray for the world and those harmed by injustice.
2. Ask God to reveal injustice you may be causing and for the strength to stop.
3. Have you unfairly judged your passport culture? How can you extend grace to it whether or not it's deserved?
4. Find a way today to stand against injustice or unfairness in a small way.

DAY 10 - JOSEPH: TRANSITION

Read Genesis 39:1-6

Key Verse: *Joseph found favor in his eyes and became his attendant. Potiphar put him in charge of his household, and he entrusted to his care everything he owned.* **Genesis 39:4**

Prayerist

Guardian, guide, no pillar of cloud by day nor fire by night, Yet I sense your presence with me,
God of the journey.
You are walking with me into a new land. You are guarding me in my vulnerable moment.
You are dwelling within me as I depart from here. You are promising to be my peace as I face the struggles . . . of distance from friends and security, the planting of feet and heart in a strange place. You will always be with me in everything. I do not know how I am being resettled, but I place my life into the welcoming arms of your love.
Encircle my heart with your peace. May your powerful presence run like a strong thread through the fibers of my being. Amen.[7]

Reflections

Joseph went through a sudden transition. He went from being the favorite son to being a slave of Potiphar, an Egyptian official. He no doubt faced painful treatment as a slave, loss of the culture he knew, and loss of his freedom. Because of the way in which he came to Egypt, Joseph could have rejected the culture and refused to adapt, but he didn't. Instead, he saw this as God's will for his life and worked at understanding the culture. Above all, God was with Joseph, granting him favor and success. If you've read the book *Holes* by Louis Sachar, you'll remember the refrain, "It's always the worst the first day" followed by "It's always the worst the second day" and so on. It seems, in fact, that each day is the worst day and that this will always be true, but it won't. Eventually it really does stop being the worst day.

Transition tends to have a wave pattern. The first few weeks are exciting; then the first months may be frustrating, difficult, or even miserable. Usually, at some point things begin to settle down and the strangeness wears off. Eventually things improve and a new normal asserts itself. But don't be surprised if sometime after that you still hit another dip. It's normal. However, this time the dip is not as deep, and people come out of it a bit faster. This pattern continues and the waves shorten until life is normal again. Knowing the pattern can help you know what to expect, be patient, and be optimistic. Also, God can give you hope and help you remember that anything is redeemable—even slavery.

Questions
- *What do you think Joseph did to help him in transition?*
- *Where in the transition pattern are you? How are you feeling in this stage?*
- *What are some things you can do to look forward to the next stage?*
- *What else is God telling you through this passage?*

Next Steps
1. Pray for smooth transitions for yourself and those around you.
2. Take time to actively imagine feeling comfortable in your new place when you have transitioned. What will it feel like? What might you do? How will your life look? How will you respond to your environment?
3. Take one step outside your comfort zone once today.

DAY 11 - JOSEPH: FITTING IN

Read Genesis 39:7-19

Key Verse: *Now Joseph was well-built and handsome, and after a while his master's wife took notice of Joseph and said, "Come to bed with me!"* **Genesis 39:6-7**

Reflections

It's challenging to adapt to a new culture. Joseph was put in charge of Potiphar's household and everything he owned. He needed to understand Egypt's economy, values, traditions, and much more. But it wasn't just the culture that Joseph encountered, it was also the Egyptian people. His role and responsibilities included interacting with Potiphar's family, employees, and other slaves. In his desire to fit into the culture, Joseph faced an important challenge. How far would he go to be accepted? When Potiphar's wife tried to seduce him, would he compromise his values? Adapting to a new culture, like Joseph did, is not an easy task. The truth is, it is difficult to blend in and become just like the locals. As you integrate into this new place, here are a few things to keep in mind.

Decisions have consequences. Things that you choose to do or not to do will affect your life in this new place and beyond. Joseph chose to refuse the advances of Potiphar's wife and the consequences were severe.

You will change. You cannot stop from changing. Whether you choose to hold onto the ways you're familiar with or learn new ones, you will change. You are growing older, you are gaining experience, and the world sees you differently now. You cannot avoid change, so be wise in choosing a good path and good people who will influence you.

You can be wrong. Not always, but sometimes. There are some things that are done better here than the ways you have done them in the past. You do not have the high ground in all topics just because you grew up internationally.

Fitting in. You may want to fit in, you may not. Either way, the standards and practices of the place you are in will inevitably shape you as you emulate them or react to them. Try to maintain a balance, neither giving up all that you are and believe, nor rejecting everything without consideration.

Expectations. Be flexible. You can't avoid having expectations; it's how our brains are wired. You need to adjust those expectations as you have new experiences.

Sometimes you must not go along. Joseph was right. In his situation he did not go with the flow, and even though he paid dearly for it, he was still right. Though it may cost you everything, sometimes adapting is wrong. Be strong; God will be with you even as He was with Joseph.

Questions

- *Which of these points are you facing most in your transition?*
- *When do you want to adapt the most? When the least? Why?*
- *What is God saying to you as you think about Joseph and his run-in with Potiphar's wife?*
- *What else is God saying to you through this passage?*

Next Steps

1. Think through the ways that your new place is asking you to change and write them down. Then choose one to try to adapt to and one to not.
2. Ask someone you trust if there are things that you should change to help you adapt to the culture.
3. List the scriptural convictions, values, and principles that you are committed to during this transition.

DAY 12 - JOSEPH: TRAPPED

Read Genesis 39:20-23

Key Verse: *Joseph's master took him and put him in prison, the place where the king's prisoners were confined.*
Genesis 39:20

31 Days of Praise - Day 17

Thank You that You have me in the place You want me just now. . . Thank You again that You meant for good the terrible things that happened to Joseph . . . and that through all this You had him in the right place at the right time, for highly important reasons. I'm glad, Lord, that You are the same today—well able to work things out for us, to turn evil into good. I stand amazed at the complexity and mystery of Your wisdom. How safe it is for me to trust Your reasons for acting (or not acting) and Your methods of working!
Thank You that I can safely commit my location and situation to You. I can "be willing for You to shift me anywhere on life's checkerboard, or bury me anywhere in life's garden, gladly yielding myself for You to please Yourself with, anywhere and anyway You choose." [8]

Reflections

Many things happened to Joseph that he never dreamed he would face. At times he might have felt he was living a nightmare. He never could have imagined being sold into slavery, taken to Egypt, or later being thrown into prison. He was trapped and there was no way out.

Like Joseph, you may be living one of your own nightmares—being stuck in your passport country. You've left a country that you probably love and have come to one that may feel strange and unfamiliar. You've said goodbye to people, some you've known for years, and may wonder if you can ever make those kinds of deep friendships here. You probably knew that at some time you would come here to start college, or perhaps you would move back when your parents' jobs changed. Now it has happened and you may feel trapped. It's normal to already be saying, "When can I leave?" or "As soon as I can, I'm out of here."

Questions

- *What are the things that are causing you to feel trapped right now?*
- *Though you can't physically move right now, what else can you do that will give you a sense of freedom?*
- *What else is God saying to you through this passage?*

Next Steps

1. Pray, asking God to help you feel content about where you are right now.
2. Name one benefit or good thing each day about being here and in this culture.

DAY 13 - JOSEPH: USING YOUR GIFTS

Read Genesis 40:1-19

Key Verse: *"We both had dreams," they answered, "but there is no one to interpret them." Then Joseph said to them, "Do not interpretations belong to God? Tell me your dreams."*
Genesis 40:8

Martin Luther

"Music is one of the fairest and most glorious gifts of God, to which Satan is a bitter enemy, for it removes from the heart the weight of sorrow, and the fascination of evil thoughts." [9]

Francis A. Shaeffer

"As a Christian we know why a work of art has value. Why? First, because a work of art is a work of creativity, and creativity has value because God is the Creator. The first sentence in the Bible is the declaration that the Creator created: 'In the beginning God created the heavens and the earth'."   *–Art and the Bible* [10]

Reflections

God gave Joseph special abilities. At times they created problems, but at other times they opened doors for him. His dreams made his brothers angry and jealous. Later on, when the famine hit, interpreting dreams saved not only his family but a nation. At times Joseph may have wondered what to do with his ability. At other times he may have said, "Why me?" Like Joseph, you have special gifts and abilities. Some of those gifts are tied to your experiences and your upbringing as TCKs. There are things you can do, things that you know, and sometimes just things that you see that are incomprehensible to those around you. Finding ways to use your gifts is likely to be a central theme of your life in the next few years.

What will you do with your gifts and abilities? Will you become conceited and make enemies because of your gift? Will you keep your gift a secret, meant for only you and God to know? Will you make friends and help people in distress? Joseph seems to have done all three at different times in his life. Remember, the gifts and abilities that make you unique are gifts from God. Trust that He will help you know how to use them. This is a goal we can all share, whether we are a TCK or not.

Questions

- *What are some of your gifts and abilities? Are they related to being a TCK or not?*
- *What are some ways you can use your gifts and abilities?*
- *Dreams and the ability to interpret them was a gift Joseph had, but he misused them when he bragged to his brothers. What is one way you could misuse your gifts or abilities?*
- *Do you ever envy another person's gift or ability?*
- *What else is God saying to you through this passage?*

Next Steps

1. Pray that God would show you your gifts and abilities and how to use them for your good and His glory.
2. Pray to be content with the gifts you've been given and be happy for others with their gifts.
3. Identify a gift in someone else today and encourage them to use it for God's kingdom.
4. Practice one of your gifts today in a way that honors God.

DAY 14 - JOSEPH: FORGOTTEN

Read Genesis 40:20-23

Key Verse: *The chief cupbearer, however, did not remember Joseph; he forgot him.* **Genesis 40:23**

Corrie ten Boom

When you are covered by His wings, it can get pretty dark. [11]

Dwight L. Moody

No matter how low down you are; no matter what your disposition has been; you may be low in your thoughts, words, and actions . . . Jesus will have compassion upon you. He will speak comforting words to you; not treat you coldly or spurn you . . . but will speak tender words, and words of love and affection and kindness. Just come at once. He is a faithful friend—a friend that sticketh closer than a brother. [12]

Reflections

Joseph not only felt trapped, but also experienced feeling forgotten and alone while in prison. New people entered his life, namely the king's cupbearer and baker. Joseph may have felt that this was his ticket to getting out of prison. Joseph interpreted the cupbearer's dream and all he asked in return was for help getting out of prison. Imagine how disappointed and alone Joseph felt when the cupbearer was released and he wasn't. Furthermore, the person he had hoped would get him out of prison completely forgot about him.

People can hurt each other, both by what we do and by what we don't do. These wounds can be deep and painful. For example, you may have friends who promised they would write or stay in touch, but they haven't, and you may feel rejected and alone. In the midst of transition, it's easy to feel alone and forgotten. While you may be feeling that way right now, God reminds us that we are never truly alone. He says of His people, "I will turn the darkness into light before them and make the rough places smooth. These are the things I will do; I will not forsake them" (Is. 42:16). Have faith in Him and be patient. In His time, He will bring new people alongside you. God sees your needs and you will not always be alone. When it feels like you are, remember He is with you and is trustworthy.

Questions
- *Have you had times during this transition when it felt like you were alone and forgotten?*
- *Did those feelings change? How and why?*
- *How did God work in your life during those times?*
- *What else is God saying to you through this passage?*

Next Steps
1. If you are alone, or are feeling alone, pray that you will have faith.
2. Pray for those who feel forgotten right now, that God will give them faith and hope.
3. Seek out someone today who may feel forgotten and show them that they are not alone.
4. When you feel really alone, ask God to show you in a tangible way that He is with you.

DAY 15 - JOSEPH: RESPONSIBILITY

Read Genesis 41:37-57

Key Verse: *You shall be in charge of my palace, and all my people are to submit to your orders. Only with respect to the throne will I be greater than you.* **Genesis 41:40**

Reflections

When Joseph was taken from his home to Egypt, he went from being a favorite son to a domestic laborer. People's expectations of him changed radically as his roles and responsibilities changed; he abruptly went from being favored to being a servant. As a slave, his body had to adjust to physical labor and his mind had to relearn what was appropriate to think.

When Joseph was thrown in prison, all of the expectations changed again. With each change Joseph had to put on the "new hats" that were expected of him. Being slave, prisoner, and eventually an important leader in Egypt meant that he continually had to adapt to each of these roles and to the expectations that went with them.

One of the most disorienting aspects of transition is the loss and re-formation of roles and responsibilities. Roles give us direction, shape our identity, and define how we interact with our community. When those roles are lost, it can be very confusing and difficult. When we give up responsibilities we've held for a long time, there can be a great sense of loss and identity confusion. However, as with Joseph, these changes can also open doors of opportunity.

As a TCK, you likely already know how different you become or how much you change depending on where you are or who you're with. Much of that change can be attributed to your roles and responsibilities. One of the great joys in transition is the ability to recast your roles and try on new responsibilities. If you were always the follower in school, now you can try to be a leader. If you were the class clown, now you can try to be the kind one. Stretching yourself with new responsibilities or in new areas, and experimenting with who you are, can be freeing. You may find that you don't necessarily fit that new persona, but having tried it, you can learn something about yourself.

Questions

- *What were your roles in your previous place? What responsibilities did you have previously? What did you enjoy and/or not enjoy about them?*
- *How would you like your new roles and responsibilities to be different in your new setting?*
- *What else is God saying to you through this passage?*

Next Steps

1. Pray that God will guide you as you pursue and develop new roles and responsibilities.
2. Find one way to try out a new role or step into new responsibilities that you want in your new place.
3. Avoid responsibilities associated with roles you would like to change.

DAY 16 - JOSEPH: GRIEF

Read Genesis 42

Key Verse: *He turned away from them and began to weep . . .*
Genesis 42:24

Reflections

Famine hit not only Egypt, but also the surrounding countries, and Joseph's brothers came looking for food. Through Joseph's leadership and planning, Egypt had stockpiled all the food it might need, and more. He met with his brothers and tested them to see if they had changed. He could have responded to them with vengeance, but instead shed tears. Joseph grieved what he had lost: his family, his culture, and years of happiness, trust, and hope. He had lost his home and childhood. You may resonate with that. Joseph's "grief tower" toppled over when seeing his brothers again. Unresolved grief can be common in the TCK experience.

Like Joseph, everyone experiences grief. But perhaps the most defining aspect of a TCK life is the grief that comes from an extremely mobile lifestyle and highly cross-cultural world. By the age of ten, most TCKs have experienced more losses than most adults, and by the time those ten-year-olds reach adulthood their grief can be crushing. Whether it's due to a lack of awareness of your own grief, a lack of permission to grieve, or simply a lack of time, grief can be delayed or ignored. But grief always comes out. Ignoring losses does not make them go away; grief can build. Many TCKs have found that later medical and emotional problems in life stem from the unresolved grief of childhood. As you make this transition, set aside real time to grieve at some point. In the words of William Shakespeare: "Give sorrow words; the grief that does not speak knits up the o-er wrought heart and bids it break."

Dealing with your grief is important for a healthy transition in more ways than one. Someone who has not grieved has a hard time bonding with new people and places. You also can't really appreciate the people and places you've loved unless you grieve for them. As long as you block off the grief, you also block away their influence and memory in your life.

Questions

- *What are some of the losses you've experienced in your last move?*
- *How do you typically process grief? Do you:*
  -try and push through it quickly?
  -ignore it?
  -allow it to pile up?
  -allow it to immobilize you?
  -receive it as a gift?
- *Do you find you grieve before a move, in the middle of a move, or after the actual move?*
- *Where are you in the grief process?*

Next Steps

1. Pray that God will help you identify the losses in your life you have yet to finish processing. Consider reading *Unstacking Your Grief Tower* by Lauren Wells.
2. Take time to write down some of the losses you have experienced. Identify someone with whom you can share them. Would counseling help?

DAY 17 - JOSEPH: REDEMPTION

Read Genesis 50

Key Verse: *You intended to harm me, but God intended it for good to accomplish what is now being done, the saving of many lives.* **Genesis 50:20**

Dan Allender

You have been damaged. But you have great hope. The mercy of God does not eradicate the damage, at least not in this life, but it soothes the soul and draws it forward to a hope that purifies and sets free. Allow the pain of the past and the travail of the change process to create fresh new life in you and to serve as a bridge over which another victim may walk from death to life.[13]

Reflections

Looking back, Joseph's life was hard. Although it was punctuated with moments of light, in general, it was a pretty depressing, and at times, hopeless story. He could have seen his brothers' treachery as unforgivable, his years as a slave as wasted, and his time as a prisoner unjust. We know these things affected him. However, this is not all Joseph concluded when he thought about his past. Joseph, a man of faith, profoundly articulated something very few of us ever even begin to understand: "What you intended for evil, God intended for good."

Joseph understood both despair and hope. You may have days when things feel hopeless: you're sick, someone in your family has cancer, you're about to fail a class, or the love of your life has walked away or just wishes you'd disappear. In times like this, you may start to wonder if God really does hear you, if He cares, or is there at all. Take heart! He is there, He is listening, and He does care.

God can redeem all things—it's His hallmark trait. No matter where you are, what you're facing, what you've done, or what's been done to you, God can redeem it. In retrospect, Joseph saw God at work in his many years of slavery and alienation from his family. At times, situations may have seemed hopeless to Joseph. God was at work in his life and is at work in your life, too. You can have faith like Joseph, knowing that there is nothing in your life that God cannot redeem—no experience, thought, feeling, or decision. Your life is in good hands!

Questions
- *What are those things in your life that seem hopeless?*
- *What do you do when you feel overwhelmed?*
- *Do you have any stories about God's redemption?*

Next Steps
1. Pray that God will give you the ability to remember His blessings when you feel hopeless.
2. Remind someone of God's redemption. Telling someone else is one of the best ways to remind ourselves.
3. Prepare a short list of God's miracles in your life and save it somewhere you can find it when you're feeling hopeless.

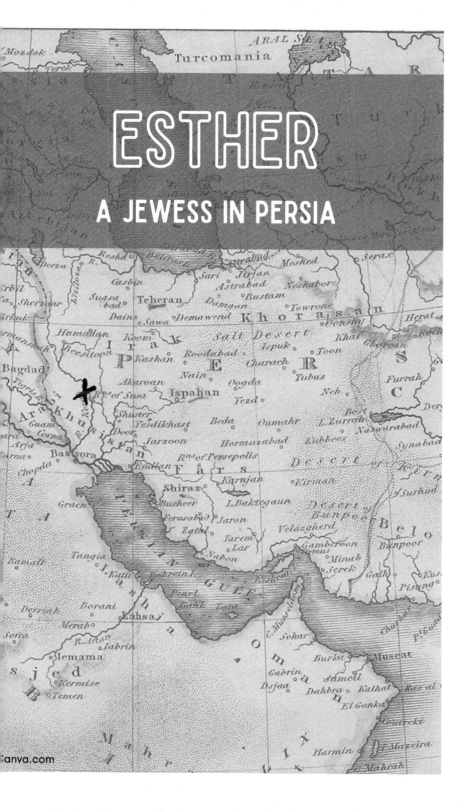

ESTHER

A JEWESS IN PERSIA

DAY 18 - ESTHER: GOD'S FAITHFULNESS

Read Esther 4:12-14

Key Verse: *And who knows but that you have come to your royal position for such a time as this?* **Esther 4:14**

Morning Prayer, Mother Teresa

May today there be peace within. May you trust God that you are exactly where you are meant to be. May you not forget the infinite possibilities that are born of faith. May you use those gifts that you have received, and pass on the love that has been given to you.

May you be content knowing you are a child of God. Let this knowledge settle into your bones, and allow your soul the freedom to sing, dance, praise and love. It is there for each and every one of us.

Reflections

"Timing is everything", they say. That was definitely true in Esther's life. She was orphaned and raised by her uncle. But her normal life was suddenly transformed by a mandatory beauty pageant. Esther "won" and consequently entered the palace, became queen, and rescued the people of Israel. She was swept up into important events, major choices, lethal risks, and God's faithfulness. God used her to change history and save the lives of thousands of God's people. There were several key turning points in her life, and they can be summarized in these words, "And who knows but that you have come . . . for such a time as this?"

When you think about your life, there have been events that changed your life forever. It may be when you went to boarding school, when a sibling nearly died, when you escaped an accident, or when civil war broke out in your country. In fact, this transition may be one of those key turning points. You may be seeing the risks, feeling the challenges, or wondering how the pieces fit together.

Just as God showed Himself faithful to Esther in the turning points of her life, He will also be faithful in yours. As we remember how He has been faithful in the past we can have confidence that He will continue to be faithful as we face the future.

Questions

- *What have been some of the key turning points in your life?*
- *How did God show His faithfulness in those events?*
- *How did God use those events in your life or in the lives of others?*
- *What else is God saying to you through this passage?*

Next Steps

1. Pray that God will show you His faithfulness during this transition.
2. Share with someone how God has been faithful to you at a turning point in your life.

DAY 19 - ESTHER: NO CHOICE

Read Esther 2:1-8

Key Verse: *When the king's order and edict had been proclaimed, many young women were brought to the citadel of Susa and put under the care of Hegai. Esther also was taken to the king's palace . . .* **Esther 2:8**

A Prayer of St. Teresa

*Govern everything by your wisdom, O Lord,
so that my soul may always be serving you
in the way you will and not as I choose.
Let me die to myself so that I may serve you;
let me live to you who are life itself. Amen.*

Reflections

Esther's parents died when she was young and her uncle, Mordecai, raised her as his own daughter. This was not a time in history when women had much choice about their lives. Hundreds of young women were taken from their homes and lives to compete in a compulsory "beauty contest" to choose a new queen. While many women may have been glad to be included, Esther didn't seek out this opportunity. She hadn't asked to move to the palace or to be part of this beauty competition. No one asked for her input; they just decided this is what she would do.

There are times when decisions are made and you don't get to be a part of the decision-making process. You may feel that you were excluded from a having a voice in something that changed your life, that no one listened to you or how you felt. Sometimes these kinds of decisions are beyond our control and they change the course of our lives. In the past it was your parents, your mission agency, a supporting church, or your school that made these decisions; now it may be college officials or employers. When you experience these moments or think back on those that have come before, take a minute to think of God. Ultimately, we can trust that no matter how poor the decisions were that people made on our behalf, God has a plan. He can and will use them for your good and His glory.

Questions

- *In making this transition, how do you feel about the voice you had in the decision?*
- *Are there emotions you are processing about a decision that was made in the past?*
- *What else is God saying to you through this passage*

Next Steps

1. Pray that God will enable you to forgive those who hurt you in how decisions were made.
2. Thank someone for listening or including your feelings/needs in a decision that was made.
3. When you find yourself in leadership, remember to include those whom you lead in decisions.

DAY 20 - ESTHER: SHARING

Read Esther 2:9-14

Key Verse: *Esther had not revealed her nationality and family background, because Mordecai had forbidden her to do so.*
Esther 2:10

Adelaide

I'm from the wide airplane wings
    Swooping me up and
setting me down.
I'm from the navy blue passport
    Filled with endless
destinations.
I'm from the suitcases not always full
    Yet always tucked away in
the corner.

I'm from the experiences, the people,
the places
    From North America to
Europe to Asia.
I'm from never knowing where I'm
from
But always feeling at home. [14]

Reflections

After months of pampering, each woman was invited to spend time with the king. Like a bad reality TV dating show, what was going to play out during their first encounter? What would they do and what would conversations even look like? Esther chose her words carefully so as not to offend her king but also not to share too much. She had been given specific instructions by Mordecai not to tell anything about her family and nationality to the king or anyone else. While it may not have seemed a big deal, it turned out to be a very important part of protecting God's people. Like Esther, you face questions about yourself and must decide what to share. It may be the question that TCKs hate, "Where are you from?" Or perhaps it isn't innocuous at all; it may be a question that delves into the heart and soul of your private life. In a new context, it is easy to go to one extreme or the other: giving too much information or hiding who you are.

Esther found a way to walk the line well. As you meet new people and get to know them, the best way to make genuine friends is to find that balance. Your stories are a part of you, but not all of you. Tell them, be real, but choose your stories carefully and share them slowly until the relationships have matured. It won't happen as quickly here as it may have in the past, but these relationships might be the ones you will carry for the rest of your life. Be intentional and invest in them.

Questions

- *How have you been approaching decisions about what to share?*
- *Do you feel that you've made mistakes in what you've shared or how you've been approaching this?*
- *Have you had experiences where you felt misunderstood or shared things you now wish you had not?*
- *What is God saying to you through this passage?*

Next Steps

1. Pray that God will give you wisdom about what, when, and how to share with others.
2. Consider answering questions with a hook in your answer so that you can evaluate people's interest and/or understanding.
3. Ask someone you've recently met and whom you trust for feedback about how you're handling these situations.

DAY 21 - ESTHER: STRESS

Read Esther 2:15-23

Key Verse: *But Mordecai found out about the plot and told Queen Esther, who in turn reported it to the king, giving credit to Mordecai.* **Esther 2:22**

Prayerist

Dear Father,
Today was one of those days—You know the ones. When life just doesn't make sense. When the world seems so unfair . . . Because it is unfair. We need You Lord. I need You. I need You to wrap your arms around me and help me understand that it's a good thing I don't understand everything. How can I possibly comprehend Your plan of the entire world? You are God. And I am not. You spoke the world into existence. You shaped humans from dust. And only You can create beauty from ashes.
Amen. [15]

Reflections

As queen, Esther found herself facing a new world and new problems. The one constant in her life was her Uncle Mordecai. He guided her as she came to the palace. He helped her deal with the king and her new life as queen. Esther faced some enormous problems and challenges, but also small ones were made more significant because she was in a new world.

As you are entering this culture, lots of day-to-day issues and problems come up. They aren't part of culture shock, but they are factors in culture stress. They are small enough that you may overlook, ignore, or forget about them in the more urgent matters of your life. It's the little things that never seem to go away that have been shown to cause more stress than even traumatic life events. The little things push you toward burnout, and so as you continue to enter into your new life you need to stop and ask yourself how you can best handle your stress.

Questions
- *Do you feel burned out?*
- *What little things in your life are rubbing at the edges of your stress?*
- *What are some practical steps you can take to reduce the little stressors in life?*
- *What else is God saying to you through this passage?*

Next Steps
1. Pray for peace that passes understanding and bring both requests and thanksgiving to God.
2. Plan out a routine to take care of one little stressor today.
3. Do one stress-reducing activity today. (Exercise, stretch, go to bed early, be grateful...)

DAY 22 - ESTHER: STANDING TOGETHER

Read Esther 4:1-17

Key Verse: *When this is done, I will go to the king, even though it is against the law. And if I perish, I perish.*
Esther 4:16

A Prayer of Help, from the Psalms

H. Hear me Lord, and answer me, for I am poor and needy. (Psalm 86:1 NIV)
E. Establish my steps in your word. (Psalm 119:133 NASB)
L. Let your compassion quickly meet our needs because we are on the brink of despair. (Psalm 79:8 NLT)
P. Protect me, God, because I take refuge in You. I say to the Lord, "You are my Lord, apart from You I have nothing good." (Psalm 16:1-2 CEB)[16]

Reflections

The stakes were very high for Esther. Success meant life for her and her people; failure meant death to everyone. As you read through Esther 4 you can hear how reluctant she was, how frightened to put her life on the line for her people. When she didn't have the courage or strength, Esther asked for help. She asked all the people to fast for her and then, armed with their support, Esther decided to take the risk. She spoke to the king and hoped she would find favor. While you probably are not facing life-and-death situations, your situations may have risks and consequences that are enormous and may have no easy solution in sight. You may be wondering where the money will come from to pay for Christmas, next semester, or next year. You may be feeling overwhelmed with homework or by classes that aren't going well. You may be trying to juggle work and school. You may even be feeling overwhelmed by feelings of homesickness, loneliness, or depression.

Esther provides a great example in dealing with these difficult situations. She sought out help and got support from positive friendships. We human beings are made with a need for other people in our lives. God calls us to a life in community, specifically a community of faith. When you find that you don't have enough courage, wisdom, or hope, reach out. The body of Christ is there for you. God heard Esther and her people. He answered her and used her to save His people. God will do the same for you. Hold fast with your family in Christ and together you will see Him be the Savior.

Questions
- *Are you facing a situation that feels like those Esther faced?*
- *How are you responding?*
- *Are you in a community that can hold you up when you need help?*
- *What else is God saying to you through this passage?*

Next Steps
1. Pray that God will guide you in the difficult situations you are facing.
2. Find another believer and ask them to pray for you.
3. Reach out for help from your RA, a professor, a teacher, or a counselor if your problem becomes bigger than you or your close community can handle.

DAY 23 - ESTHER: CONVICTIONS

Read Esther 7:1-10

Key Verse: *Then Queen Esther answered, "If I have found favor with you, Your Majesty, and if it pleases you, grant me my life—this is my petition. And spare my people—this is my request."* **Esther 7:3**

Rachel Britton

Lord God, I want to not only have the courage to act quickly when I need to, but also to make sure my actions are right and pleasing in your eyes. I ask you to give me the wisdom to know when to act quickly to do the right thing. When I can avert disaster whether at home or across the world, show me how to act wisely. When I can stop others doing the wrong thing . . . give me the courage to step up and speak. When I need to do the right thing that goes against the norms of today, give me common sense, and integrity. Lord, thank you for your wisdom that you give to those who ask. I ask you in advance to give me wisdom when needed. Fill me with humility and courage to do the right thing quickly. In Jesus' name. Amen.[17]

Reflections

Courage is prominent in the story of Esther. Esther stood up for her people, risking her own life to face the king. She may have thought that someone else should go to the king, that someone else would be better to take Haman's plans forward. But Esther's courage showed her faith and confidence in the wisdom of her Uncle Mordecai and in the God of her people. The timing of this was important. This kind of bravery might not have been possible when she first arrived, but Esther had become accustomed to the palace and its ways. She had matured and was ready to stand up for her people. She not only needed courage, but cultural understanding and confidence. This can be a very important issue for you now. Sometimes when people have taken a stand on certain political, social, or spiritual issues, they've given very negative impressions. Topics like abortion, homosexuality, or even faith can carry the risk of being given permanent labels like intolerant, homophobic, or narrow-minded. Sometimes TCKs stand up for unpopular countries or people when the media gives slanted portrayals.

What will you stand for and how will you do it? Esther stood up for her people in a redemptive and culturally appropriate way. She didn't do it to shock, to provoke, to anger, or to get revenge. She courageously stood up for the needs of others. Led by the Holy Spirit, you can take a stand for faith and truth that have the power to change the world.

Questions
- *As you've transitioned, what things have you taken a stand on?*
- *How have you done that?*
- *How have others responded to what you've said and done?*
- *What does it look like to wait to stand until you are better prepared?*
- *What else is God saying to you through this passage?*

Next Steps
1. Ask someone how people disagree respectfully where you live.
2. Write down areas you want to take a stand for. Write down areas you are willing to wait on.
3. Pray that God will give you wisdom as you stand up for things both in what you stand for, as well as how you do it.

DAY 24 - ESTHER: BROKENNESS

Read Esther 8:1-17

Key Verse: *For how can I bear to see disaster fall on my people? How can I bear to see the destruction of my family?*
Esther 8:6

Elisabeth Elliot

*We want to avoid suffering, death, sin, ashes.
But we live in a world crushed and broken and
torn, a world God Himself visited to redeem.
We receive His poured-out life, and being
allowed the high privilege of suffering with Him,
may then pour ourselves out for others.* [18]

Reflections

Haman hated the Jews. Prejudice and racism was not surprising in Esther's time and should not be a surprise today. Esther had to deal with it in Haman and probably feared that the king himself would share Haman's prejudice. Throughout Scripture we see examples of God's people suffering from and confronting prejudice towards the Jews, Samaritans, women, the sick, and the poor. They were persecuted, oppressed, demeaned, and hated. Choosing to stand up for the oppressed was often a quick way to end up oppressed yourself.

You may or may not have experienced prejudice and racism yourself, but you'll likely face some version of it in your college experience. You may be frustrated by the lack of ethnic or cultural diversity on your campus. You might be used to seeing faces of many colors, many socioeconomic levels, or people with different religious backgrounds. But those around you might seem homogenous; you may hear comments that hurt or offend you, or perhaps something important will be going on back in your country and no one will seem to care.

Your experience will make you more sensitive to the prejudice and racism in the world around you. This is a gift, as difficult as it may seem. You have unique freedom from some of the assumptions and prejudice that those around you may be caught in. However, be careful as you exercise this gift. God has given you the ability to see brokenness. Be gentle as you address the hurt of the world, even as Jesus was with us.

Questions

- *Have you seen or experienced instances of racism and prejudice?*
- *How have you responded?*
- *What else is God saying to you through this passage?*

Next Steps

1. Pray for the oppressed and marginalized all over the world.
2. Plan how you will react the next time you are surprised or hurt by prejudice.

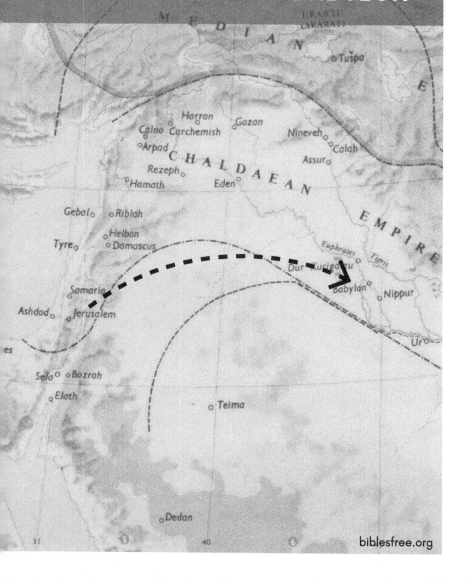

DANIEL

FROM JERUSALEM TO BABYLON

DAY 25 - DANIEL: CULTURAL VALUES

Read Daniel 6:21-22

Key Verse: *They have not hurt me, because I was found innocent in his sight. Nor have I ever done any wrong before you, Your Majesty.* **Daniel 6:22**

A Prayer of St. Francis

Lord, make me an instrument of Your peace; Where there is hatred, let me sow love; Where there is injury, pardon; Where there is discord, harmony; Where there is error, truth; Where there is doubt, faith; Where there is despair, hope; Where there is darkness, light; And where there is sadness, joy.

O Divine Master, grant that I may not so much seek To be consoled as to console; To be understood as to understand; To be loved as to love. For it is in giving that we receive; It is in pardoning that we are pardoned; And it is in dying that we are born to eternal life.

Reflections

Throughout his life, Daniel confronted enormous challenges. While he was still very young, Daniel survived a siege by the enemies of Judah and was carried off to Babylon, leaving his land and family behind—if they were even alive. Thrust from chaos to chaos Daniel had his faith and life threatened from the moment he arrived at the king's palace. As Scripture shows us, Daniel faced risk after risk from things as seemingly innocent as food to the ultimate crime of praying to God. It seems everywhere Daniel turned, danger lurked nearby.

As if it wasn't hard enough to face all of these challenges, Daniel did this while separated from his home in Jerusalem and his family. Daniel experienced the benefits of living in Babylon, learning language, literature, and culture. But the values of Babylon were at odds with the culture and values of his Jewish heritage. Time and time again, Daniel faced value conflicts and had to decide what values he would discard and what ones he would hold onto as more precious than even life itself.

Questions
- *What value differences have you experienced between your host and passport cultures?*
- *How have you handled or responded to the value differences?*
- *Have you been a bridge between cultures in any way?*
- *What else is God saying to you through this passage?*

Next Steps
1. Pray for wisdom to know how to respond when your values are challenged.
2. Pray for discernment to know the difference between cultural values and biblical values.
3. Look for an opportunity today where you can be a culture bridge.

DAY 26 - DANIEL: NEW NAMES

Read Daniel 1:1-7

Key Verse: *The chief official gave them new names: to Daniel, the name Belteshazzar; to Hananiah, Shadrach; to Mishael, Meshach; and to Azariah, Abednego.* **Daniel 1:7**

C. S. Lewis

Lucy and Edmund, when asked if he (Aslan) was here in our world as well:

"Are—are you there too, Sir?" said Edmund.

"I am," said Aslan. "But there I have another name. You must learn to know me by that name. This was the very reason why you were brought to Narnia, that by knowing me here for a little, you may know me better there."

-*Voyage of the Dawn Treader*[19]

Reflections

When Daniel and his friends arrived in their new land, they were each given a new name. He went from being Daniel to being Belteshazzar. He didn't choose his name; it was given to him by people who had been enemies. That name was meant to help them adapt and begin a new life. They were to become Babylonians, no longer to be Jews. However, there's much more to a name than just a word. Your name is the expression of your identity. As we know, the Babylonians' plans didn't completely work or fail. Daniel and his three friends did become skilled in the language, literature, and the culture of the Babylonians. They took on new identities and thrived. They learned the ropes of their new world and Daniel eventually became one of the most powerful men in the empire. But while their identities had been changed, they had not been lost. They never forgot who they were, nor did they try to hide their old identity. Their example is a fantastic one to emulate.

As you move into your new place, remember that you will never fully lose who you were, nor can you fully remain as that person either. This new place requires a whole life to fill it and not half a life here, and half there. You need to find ways to live here and to give yourself fully to life here. Take on the new life and discover how God plans for you to "have life, and have it to the full" (John 10:10) in this new location.

Questions

- What are some things you bring with you from your old life and culture?
- What do you think it means for you to take a new name in your new place? Does it mean a new way of looking at yourself, or literally a new name to call yourself? Can you give it to yourself or does it have to come from the people in the new land?
- What does a full life mean? What are the individual parts of that whole life

Next Steps

1. Pray that God would guide you to the places in your new life where you need to commit.
2. Pray that God would guide you as you choose what to hold onto from your past, and what to let go.
3. Whatever it looks like for you to take on a new name, consider taking steps towards it so that you can live more fully in your new place.

DAY 27 - DANIEL: GAME PLAN

Read Daniel 1:8-21

Key Verse: *The king talked with them, and he found none equal to Daniel, Hananiah, Mishael and Azariah; so they entered the king's service.* **Daniel 1:19**

Prayerist

Heavenly Father, I feel that I am stepping out onto the threshold of a completely new beginning with a total change in my lifestyle. Lord, I know that this is a wonderful opportunity that You have graciously opened up for me and I pray that You would be with me to lead and guide, as I seek to become accustomed to so many changes in my life.

I pray that You would remain ever close to me, and that I do not stray far from Your side or become lukewarm in my attitude towards the things of God. Help me to keep my eyes firmly fixed on Jesus and to trust all I say and do into Your capable hands. Provide, I pray, all that I need to carry out the tasks and duties that I am called upon to do with grace and courage, and I pray that my joy would be firmly fixed in Jesus and that I may be strengthened with all power from above. In Jesus' name I pray, Amen. [20]

Reflections

After being taken by force to Babylon, Daniel and his three friends surprised people by choosing not to violate God's commands by eating the king's food. They insisted on a test: their different and healthier diet against the rest of the king's servants. To the shock of the king's servants, Daniel and his friends exceeded expectations, looked healthier, and found favor in the eyes of the king's officials. They passed the test and were given privileged positions in Babylon that allowed them to become people of importance in their new world. As you transition to your passport country, like Daniel you bring with you skills, attitudes, experiences, and perspectives that have prepared you in ways that may surprise some of the people you meet. In dealing with the officials in Babylon, Daniel demonstrated honesty, hard work, respect, courage, and obedience. These are qualities that are often in short supply today that many people don't have. However, like Daniel you can have these qualities, and when they are demonstrated they can set you above the rest, whether that's the workforce, classroom, or community. Emphasize the positive aspects of your upbringing and heritage as a TCK. It will help set you up for greater success as you transition.

Questions

- *What are some of the skills or attitudes that you were raised with that can be advantageous in your transition?*
- *How can you use those advantages in the social, work, and academic areas of life?*
- *Daniel and his friends had to forgo "great" food to excel and appropriately adapt to their new culture. What part(s) of this culture may you need to forgo while adapting to the culture?*

Next Steps

1. Pray that God will maximize your advantages and minimize your disadvantages in this transition, and that you would remember to give Him the glory for it.
2. Choose three things that you can use as your countercultural advantages.
3. List the things you will have to avoid or give up in order to gain or maintain those advantages. Then think about what the things you gave up accomplished for you (socially, physically, emotionally, spiritually, etc.) and list ways you can accomplish the same things in different ways later.

DAY 28 - DANIEL: FACING THE FIRE

Read Daniel 3:1-30

Key Verse: *They saw that the fire had not harmed their bodies, nor was a hair of their heads singed; their robes were not scorched, and there was no smell of fire on them.*
Daniel 3:27

Elisabeth Elliot

Loving Lord and heavenly Father, I offer up today all that I am, all that I have, all that I do, and all that I suffer, to be Yours today and Yours forever. Give me grace, Lord, to do all that I know of Your holy will.
Purify my heart, sanctify my thinking, correct my desires.

Teach me, in all of today's work and trouble and joy, to respond with honest praise, simple trust, and instant obedience, that my life may be in truth a living sacrifice, by the power of Your Holy Spirit and in the name of Your Son Jesus Christ, my Master and my all.

Amen.

Reflections

Daniel's friends literally faced the fire. The king built a golden image and ordered that everyone bow down and worship it. The consequence for disobedience was being thrown into a blazing furnace. Daniel's friends refused to worship anyone but God and were therefore thrown into the furnace. Just before being thrown in they told the king that God would save them, but that even if He didn't, they would not bow down. Miraculously, God protected them in the furnace and spared their lives. The king was so awed that he prohibited anyone from speaking against God, and he promoted the young Jewish men. Sometimes we get tossed into the fire too. Not literally, but sometimes what you are facing can seem as painful and dangerous as fire. The thing about fire is that there is really no way to defend yourself. In transitioning to a new culture, things happen where there is no way to prepare. You are sometimes clueless about how things are supposed to work and you step blindly into a fire.

When it feels like you are facing the fire, remember Romans 8:35-39. There are many benefits to being a TCK. Your life has uniquely prepared you to face many upcoming challenges that a monocultural life likely would not. However, in transition you may face situations with enormous risks—physically, emotionally, or spiritually. Your status as an outsider, your limited knowledge of the culture, or your personal beliefs may cause you to make choices that have lasting consequences. When the fire is on, remember that there is only one person that can save you, and nothing can separate you from Him.

Questions

- *What situations may you face (or have already faced) that put you at risk because of the potential long-term consequences?*
- *Are there areas in your life where you are vulnerable to physical, emotional, or spiritual risks?*
- *Who are the people you can rely on when you find yourself facing fire?*

Next Steps

1. Pray for those who, this very day, are being persecuted for their faith in Jesus Christ.
2. Take steps to address areas in your life where you are at risk or are vulnerable.
3. Be available to be an angel in the midst of somebody else's fiery furnace.

DAY 29 - DANIEL: PRAYER

Read Daniel 9:1-19

Key Verse: *Lord, listen! Lord, forgive! Lord, hear and act!*
For your sake, my God, do not delay, because your city and
your people bear your Name. **Daniel 9:19**

Elisabeth Elliot

Prayer lays hold of God's plan and becomes the link between his will and its
accomplishment on earth. Amazing things happen, and we are given the
privilege of being the channels of the Holy Spirit's prayer.

Andrew Murray

Prayer is not monologue, but dialogue; God's voice is its most essential part.
Listening to God's voice is the secret of the assurance that he will listen to mine.

Charles Stanley

Since God knows our future, our personalities, and our capacity to listen, he
isn't ever going to say more to us than we can deal with at the moment.[21]

Reflections

Daniel recognized the needs and issues of his people, and he was in a position to affect things. Daniel had reputation, power, and position that he could have easily relied on to solve his people's problems. But Daniel took a very different approach. Instead of relying on himself, Daniel pled with God in prayer and fasting. He confessed the sins of his people and begged for mercy. Our prayers tend to be different. "Please let me pass that test! Oh God, I'd do anything if you'd make her go out with me. Dear Lord, will you please help my cold to go away?" These are the prayers that fill our lives. From childhood we've heard the saying that "God is not a vending machine to run to just with our requests". We've heard it and we know it, but sometimes, if we're honest, we feel a little guilty because we know that's often the primary focus of our prayers. While God does care about these issues, prayer can be so much more.

During times of transition we constantly feel our need for God's help. We know that we ought to be praying for others, but it seems like there's never enough time or energy for selfless prayers. However, it's at times like this when we especially need to be praying for others. Praying for the needs of others, for the world, and for His kingdom opens our eyes to the bigger picture of God's plan. It puts our lives in perspective so that we see that our problems, as insurmountable as they may seem, are small and light (2 Cor 4:17) in the scope of the eternal things.

Questions

- *What role is prayer playing in your life as you transition? Are the challenges of transition encouraging you to pray, or are they keeping you from praying?*
- *What are you praying about? Is your prayer focused on you?*
- *What broader things might God be calling you to pray for?*

Next Steps

1. Pray the Lord's Prayer and substitute the traditional phrases to needs that God is putting on your heart. For example, "Thy kingdom come" becomes "God, please bring your kingdom to war-torn Africa, the Middle East, the church in America, etc."
2. When something good happens today, thank God right then and there.
3. When you see someone in trouble today, or looking stressed, pray for them.

DAY 30 - DANIEL: FRIEND OF GOD

Read Daniel 6

Key Verse: *The king was overjoyed and gave orders to lift Daniel out of the den. And when Daniel was lifted from the den, no wound was found on him, because he had trusted in his God.* **Daniel 6:23**

Jerry Bridges

Any time we are tempted to doubt God's love for us, we should go back to the Cross. We should reason somewhat in this fashion: If God loved me enough to give His Son to die for me when I was His enemy, surely He loves me enough to care for me now that I am His child. Having loved me to the ultimate extent of the Cross, He cannot possibly fail to love me in my times of adversity. Having given such a priceless gift as His Son, surely He will also give all else that is consistent with His glory and my good. [22]

Reflections

Daniel had one of the closest relationships with God of any person in Scripture. He was one of King Darius' top administrators. He had many responsibilities, faced enormous demands on his time, and there were people who were out to get him. Yet he still managed to pray three times a day. His faith was central in his life. It showed up in his language when he talked about "my God" in verse 21. Daniel's faith was tied to his identity as we see in the king's words, "May your God whom you serve continually, rescue you" in verse 16. It was this deep faith and relationship with God that saved Daniel from a den of lions.

How is your relationship with God as you are transitioning to life in your passport country? Recently you've met lots of people and started new relationships. It's easy to forget that our faith is, in essence, a relationship. When you make a friend, what does that friend want from you, or what do you want from them? Time, talking, and doing things together are important to making a good friendship. Treat God like a person and build that relationship with Him. It may seem like hard work at times. You may experience awkward pauses in the conversation or feel that you don't understand what God is doing . . . just as you would in any human relationship. Investing in your relationship with God is difficult, but it is the most rewarding experience you can ever have. He is the best friend, wisest mentor, and greatest master you could ever imagine. Make him your best friend as Daniel did. You won't regret it.

Questions
- *Like Daniel, are there people or circumstances that are threatening or undermining your relationship with God? How are you responding?*
- *How central is your relationship with God to your daily life, reputation, or identity?*
- *What else is God saying to you through this passage?*

Next Steps
1. Invite God on an outing with you such as a walk or a bike ride.
2. When something exciting or awful happens and you need to tell someone, tell Him first.
3. Identify one step that you can take to strengthen your relationship with God.

Acknowledgement Page

This book could not have come together without **Janet Blomberg**'s vision and desire to help MKs/TCKs connect to their faith while they experience cross-cultural transition. Hundreds of TCKs benefited from this work in an earlier email format. We hope she will be encouraged to see it made available to a wider audience.

David Abernathy's editing and applicable biblical scholarship were an immeasurable help. He kept *Faith on the Move* accurate and non-heretical. He loves the Oxford comma—which endears him to writers everywhere.

Dane Stevenson created the original email layout of this work. We're thankful for the foundation he created for this book.

Holly Baldwin took it to the next level by creating layouts and consistent formatting for publication. She also graciously fixed things we accidentally moved and reformatted many, many times.

Mindy Taylor proofread, researched new quotes, fed and watered us, all while cheering us on to completion.

To the MKs/TCKs on our TCK Connect calls, from Transit Lounge and all the others we have had the privilege to journey with, we pushed this across the finish line with you in mind.

Sheryl O'Bryan and Bret Taylor
Skyping from Somewhere on the Eastern Seaboard of the United States,
March 2022

Sources

Ruth

    Day 2 [1] Myers, Ruth, and Warren Myers. *31 Days of Praise: Enjoying God Anew.* Page 81. Multnomah Books, 2005.

    Day 3 [2] Herringshaw, Mark, and Jill Herringshaw. 2017. beliefnet.com, accessed 22 February 2022, <https://www.beliefnet.com/columnists/prayerplainandsimple/2017/10/prayer-find-real-friend.html>

    Day 4 [3] accessed 22 February 2022 <https://prayerist.com/prayer/mourningloss>

    Day 5 [4] Hedrick, Misty. 2021. Lifeway.com, accessed 22 February 2022, <https://research.lifeway.com/2021/03/24/5-ways-the-church-can-serve-gen-z-women>

    Day 6 [5] Shirey, Kathryn. 2019. prayerandpossibilities.com, accessed 22 Februrary 2022, <https://www.prayerandpossibilities.com/prayer-for-families>

Joseph

    Day 7 [6] Oswald Chambers. *My Utmost for His Highest*, Westwood, NJ: Barbour and Company, 1935.

    Day 10 [7] Prayerist.com accessed 22 February 2022, <https://prayerist.com/prayer/movingaway>

    Day 12 [8] Myers, Ruth, and Warren Myers. *31 Days of Praise: Enjoying God Anew.* Multnomah Books, 2005.

    Day 13 [9] Martin Luther - christianquotes.info, accessed 22 February 2022, <https://www.christianquotes.info/quotes-by-topic/quotes-about-gifts>

    [10] Francis A. Shaeffer - goodreads.com, accessed 22 February 2022, <https://www.goodreads.com/work/quotes/963387-art-and-the-bible>

    Day 14 [11] Corrie ten Boom quoteambition.com, accessed 22 February 2022,<https://www.quoteambition.com/corrie-ten-boom-quotes>

    [12] Dwight L. Moody christianquotes.info, accessed 23 February 2022, <https://www.christianquotes.info/top-quotes/14-comforting-quotes-about-loneliness>

Joseph continued

Day 17 [13] Allender, Dan. *The Wounded Heart: Hope for Adult Victims of Childhood Sexual Abuse*, Colorado Springs, CO: NavPress, 1990.

Esther

Day 20 [14] Gardner, Marilyn, communicatingacrossboundaries.com, accessed 23 February 2022 <https://communicatingacrossboundariesblog.com/2014/08/26/im-from>

Day 21 [15] Prayerist.com, accessed 22 February 2022, <https://prayerist.com/prayer/transition>

Day 22 [16] Justdisciple.com, accessed 23 February 2022, <https://justdisciple.com/christian-prayer-help>

Day 23 [17] Britton, Rachel. biblestudytools.com, accessed 23 February 2022, <https://www.biblestudytools.com/bible-study/topical-studies/prayers-for-courage-to-do-the-right-thing.html>

Day 24 [18] Christianquotes.info. accessed 23 February 2022, <https://www.christianquotes.info/quotes-by-topic/quotes-about-brokenness>

Daniel

Day 26 [19] Lewis, C. S. *The Voyage of the Dawn Treader*, New York: Macmillan. 1952.

Day 27 [20] Prayerist.com, accessed 22 February 2022, <https://prayerist.com/prayer/movingtoanewlocation>

Day 29 [21] Thelife.com, accessed 23 February 2022, <https://thelife.com/great-quotes-on-prayer>

Day 30 [22] Bridges, Jerry. *Trusting God*. Colorado Springs, CO: NavPress, 1988.

A third culture kid (TCK) is an individual who, having spent a significant part of their development years in a culture other than their parents' home culture, develops a sense of relationship to all of the cultures, while not having full ownership in any. Elements from each culture are incorporated into the life experience, but the sense of belonging is in relationship to others of similar experience.

- DAVID C. POLLOCK

Learn more about Third Culture Kids at Interaction International

INTER/ACTION
INTERNATIONAL

www.interactionintl.org
office@interactionintl.org